E320084799

AF469288

Nottinghamshire County Council **Community Services**	
PETERS	24-May-2012
646.72	£12.99

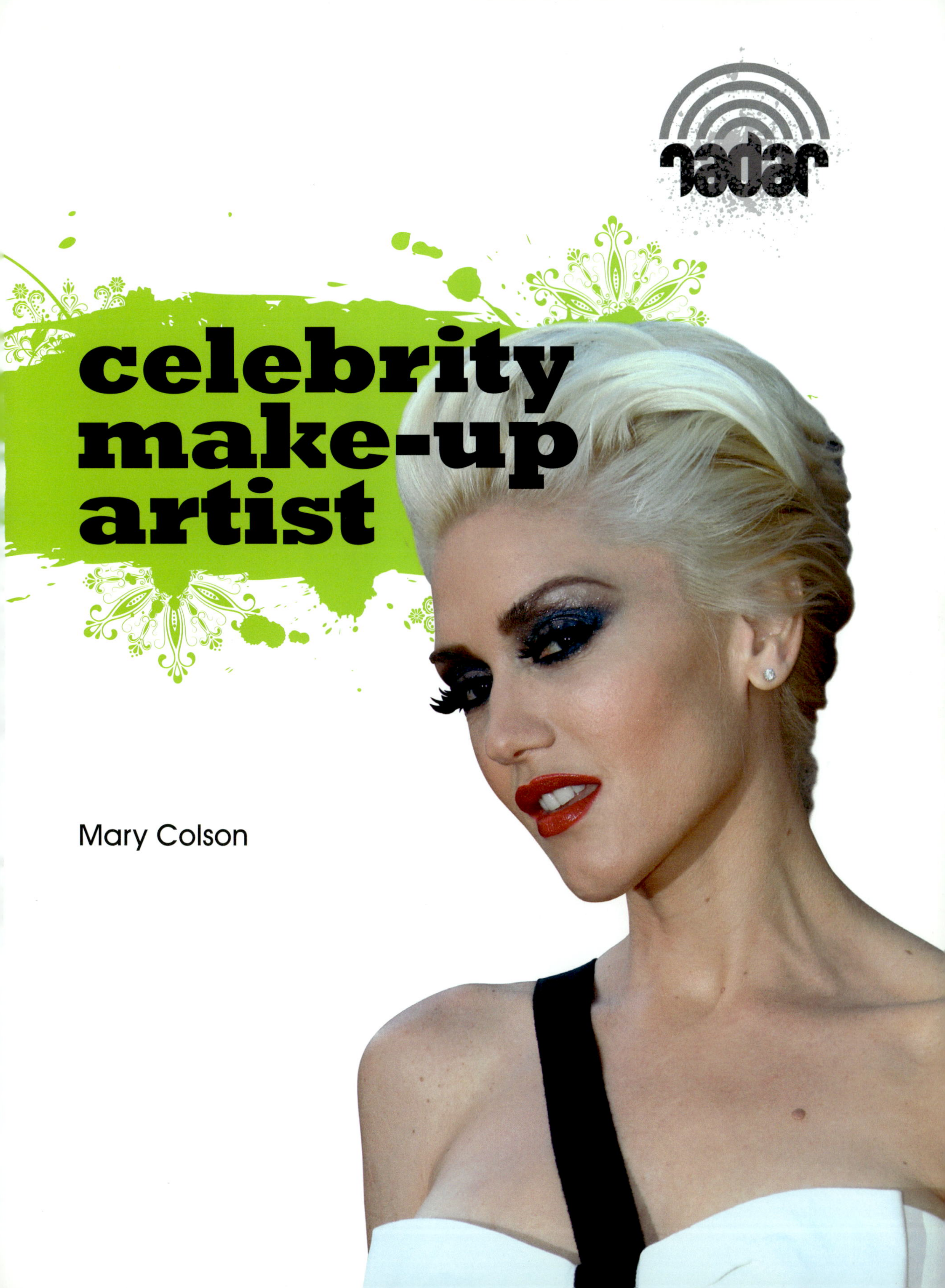

radar
celebrity make-up artist
Mary Colson

First published in 2012 by Wayland

Copyright © Wayland 2012

Wayland
Hachette Children's Books
338 Euston Road
London NW1 3BH

Wayland Australia
Level 17/207 Kent Street
Sydney NSW 2000

Concept by Joyce Bentley

Commissioned by Debbie Foy and
Rasha Elsaeed

Produced for Wayland by Calcium
Designer: Paul Myerscough
Editor: Sarah Eason

Photographer: Meg Hawkins

British Library Cataloguing in Publication Data

Celebrity make-up artist. — (Top jobs)(Radar)
   1. Makeup artists—Juvenile literature.
   I. Series
   646.7'2'092-dc23

ISBN: 978 0 7502 6462 4

Every effort has been made to clear copyright.
Should there be any inadvertent omission, please
apply to the publisher for rectification.

Printed in China

Wayland is a division of Hachette Children's Books,
an Hachette UK company.

www.hachette.co.uk

Acknowledgements: Myriam Djellouli: 2c, 25;
Julian Watson Agency: 16, 16–17; Cassie
Lomas: 2b, 6l, 6–7, 7r; Mitsuki McCormack: 8b,
29b; Rex: FoxSearch/Everett 12; Shutterstock:
Subbotina Anna 14–15, cinemafestival 1, 31br,
Olga Ekaterincheva 27, Helga Esteb 15, 18,
21, 29tl, 29tc, 31tr, Raisa Kanareva 9br,
krivenko 3br, Luba V Nel 8t, PhotoStock10 9l,
Joe Seer 3bl, 4–5, 30–31, Gina Smith 9tr,
stocklight cover, 10tl, 22t, Valua Vitaly 20,
Carla Van Wagoner 29tr, Vladimir Wrangel 26.

cover stories

10, 22
SHOW ME
Create your own red carpet looks
with the Radar make-over guide!

24 REAL LIFE STORY
Discover what it's like to
be a real life star maker!

30
TOP FIVE
The best make-up
tricks in the business

6
BLOG SPOT
A week in the life of celebrity
make-up artist Cassie Lomas

thepeople

theart

thetalk

Glamorous stars tread Hollywood's red carpet, actors light up the big screen and celebrities fill the glossy pages of magazines. But who is behind their flawless looks?

A-LIST LOOKS

Lights, camera – sparkle!

Celebrity make-up artists are responsible for improving and maximising a star's look so that they shine in the spotlight.

Make-up artists work in film and TV, making up actors to create their character's look. They also make up other famous people, including celebrities, politicians and members of the royal family. Make-up artists ensure their clients can be photographed with hundreds of flashing bulbs while still looking great.

The jet set

Make-up artists work on film and TV sets, in theatre productions, and at the world's fashion shows in countless locations, from Paris (France) and London (UK), to New York (USA) and Tokyo (Japan). A-list celebrities know the value of a top make-up artist. Many even fly their favourite artist to wherever they are in the world to create a look for a photo shoot or important appearance, such as a film prémiere.

Making it

To be a great make-up artist, you don't need to be good at art or able to draw, but you do need a strong sense of colour, style and imagination. On top of that, you need a shedload of practice, luck and if you want to make it to the top, a real passion for the job.

Macho make-up

Make-up artists work on male celebrities, too. Stars such as Ben Stiller, Johnny Depp and Robert Pattinson have their faces worked on before they go on a film set, appear on TV or make an entrance at an awards ceremony.

A week in the life of a celebrity make-up artist

CASSIE LOMAS

Monday

There has been no routine whatsoever to my life as a make-up artist! Last year, I toured with Lady Gaga for six months. Being away from home was hard. This year I am focusing on teaching students at my make-up academy. I started the academy from scratch, so it has taken all my energy to make it a success.

Tuesday

I left home in Manchester, UK, at 7am and got the train to London to work on a chat show. On the train, I caught up on some research. I have done a lot of work on fashion shoots for magazines such as Glamour, Marie Claire and Grazia, and before each shoot I researched ideas to try out. I got to the studios at 12pm, did hair and make-up for two hours. We wrapped at 4pm, after the show had been filmed.

blog   news   events

Wednesday

At 8am, I left home to work on the set for a new TV show. I was a guest on the show as the make-up artist creating new looks for women. We wrapped at 7pm, but I didn't get home until midnight – I fell straight into bed, I was so tired!

Thursday

It was photo shoot day at the academy. This meant the students were presenting their make-up designs on real models for the first time. There were students, models and make-up kits everywhere! It was a real buzz!

Friday

I spent the day filming more episodes of the new show. Call time on the show was 7am, so I was up before 6am to get myself ready. We wrapped at 3pm. On the train home, I checked my emails and returned calls.

Saturday

I taught a basic beauty course at the academy all day. You have to be dedicated in this business: my work has always come first, so I've never had a lot of time off!

Sunday

I managed to have some down-time and a family dinner today – a rare treat! I don't mind though, my job is amazing and I wouldn't want to do anything else.

THE LOOKS

Make-up is much more than a touch of lipstick or a dab of powder. From celebrity glamour and catwalk cool to award-winning film and TV faces, make-up artists work in many different fields to create the outrageous, the extravagant and the extraordinary.

Camera and catwalk

Catwalk and photographic make-up is more dramatic and thickly applied than the make-up looks created for TV, film or an awards ceremony. Some of the most dramatic looks are seen on the catwalk and in make-up launch photoshoots. For its 2011 range launch, make-up giant MAC turned its back on traditional looks and hired revolutionary make-up artist Cindy Sherman to design the looks for its advertising campaign. Cindy made up model's faces to look like clowns, with white faces, exaggerated eyebrows and huge, brightly-coloured lips.

Looking the part

Stage make-up or 'cake' has to be seen from a distance and under bright lights, so it is thickly applied or 'caked on'. Theatrical make-up helps to create different characters, from white-faced, red-lipped pantomime dames to dark-eyed tragic heroes.

Changing bodies

Prosthetics are artificial latex shapes that are used to change appearances such as the shape of a nose. Larger prosthetics can create weird and wonderful aliens and monsters.

Call 999!

Fake blood powder, plastic bone bits, stick-on scars and sweat drops are in every film set make-up kit. Using these products, make-up artists can recreate everything, from accidents and operations to murder victims. Some of the most inventive make-up work takes place on thriller or horror film sets.

Catwalk make-up (above and top right) is often highly dramatic and designed to help create a 'story' that compliments the designer's clothing range.

Stage make-up helps to create a 'character' and is heavily applied so that it is visible from a distance.

Visit www.lightbox.time.com and type in 'Cindy Sherman' to see MAC's exciting looks.

AMAZING EYES!

Recreate Rihanna's look! Follow the step-by-step guide to smoky eyes, then complete the look with the gorgeous lips guide on pages 22–23.

You will need:
• pale grey eyeshadow
• dark grey eyeshadow
• 2 eyeshadow brushes
• black eye pencil and mascara

1 Use a pale grey eyeshadow to cover the whole of the eyelid from lash line to eyebrow.

2 Dip another brush into the dark grey eyeshadow and use it to shade along the lash line.

10

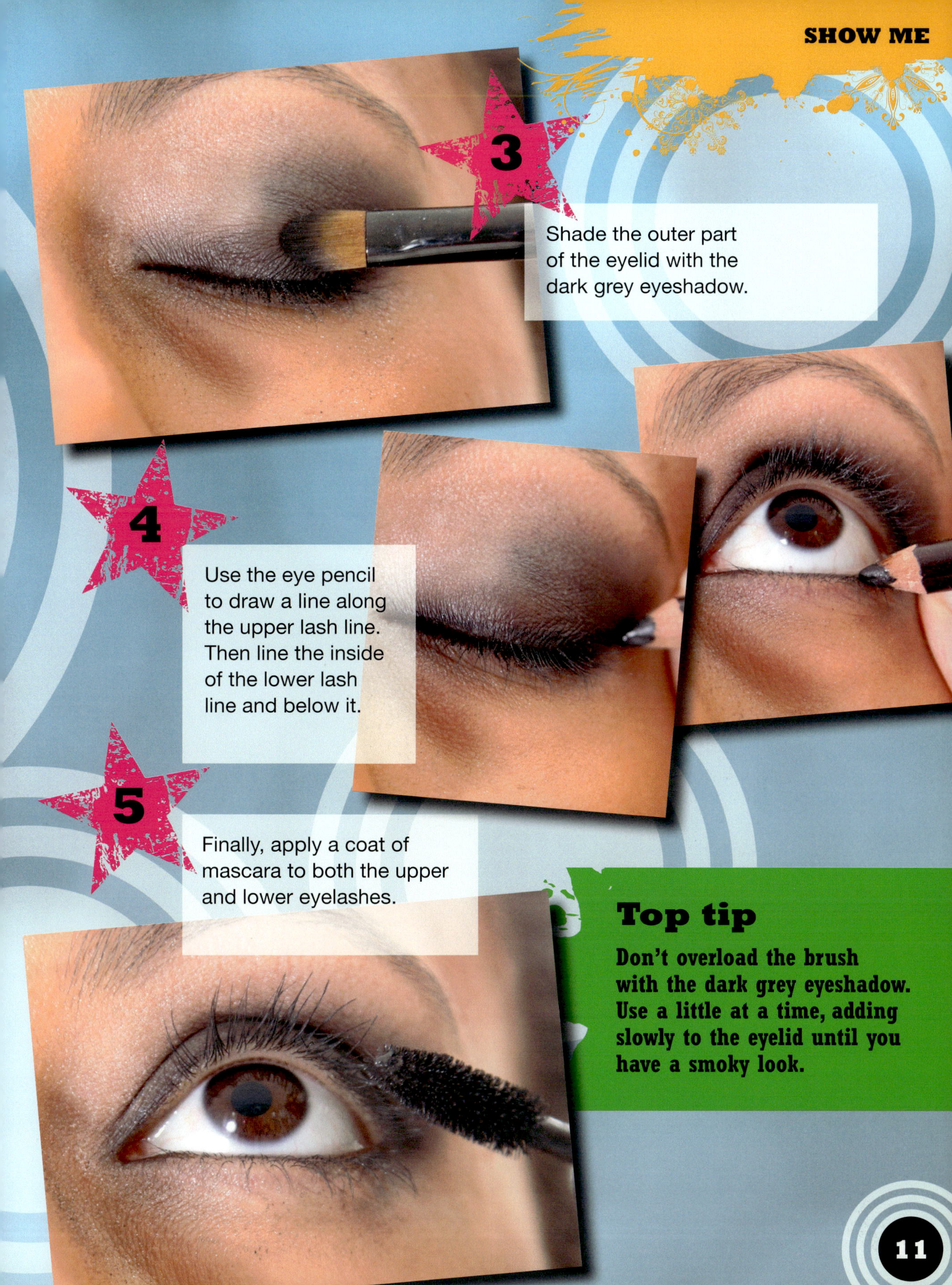

3 Shade the outer part of the eyelid with the dark grey eyeshadow.

4 Use the eye pencil to draw a line along the upper lash line. Then line the inside of the lower lash line and below it.

5 Finally, apply a coat of mascara to both the upper and lower eyelashes.

Top tip

Don't overload the brush with the dark grey eyeshadow. Use a little at a time, adding slowly to the eyelid until you have a smoky look.

JUDY CHIN
Make-up's leading lady
When Judy designed the looks for *Black Swan* (2010), she used dramatic make-up to convey the dark side of Natalie Portman's character.
Type 'black swan Klaire Delys' into www.youtube.com to see a fantastic step-by-step make-up tutorial.
12

Painting with make-up

Judy studied fine art and film at college and in 1988, she moved to New York City, USA. She took a job at the New York City Opera, where she spent four years creating looks for the dancers and developing her stage make-up skills. Judy soon discovered that she could use make-up to create a sense of the dancer's stage character.

An artist at work

Judy's screen career began in the early-1990s, when she worked on the TV show *Monsters*. Judy believed that make-up could 'create an emotion or a feeling' as well as an image, and drew portraits of the characters she made up to establish their personality and mood. She soon became famous for the great attention she gave to the fine details that could convey aspects of a character's personality.

Into film

Judy's artistry was soon in demand in the film world where her talent was showcased in productions such as *Fred Claus* (2007) and *Jumper* (2008). Judy also became the personal make-up artist to actress Sarah Jessica Parker on many films, including *Failure to Launch* (2006).

THE STATS

Name: Judy Chin
Job: Make-up artist
Personal status: Married, one son
Lucky break: Working for New York City Opera

Film star's favourite

Judy is constantly in demand with directors and actors alike. Her sense of design and her understanding of character are what make stars such as Sarah Jessica Parker, Ben Stiller and Rachel Weisz ask for her time after time.

Career highlights

2000–2010 personal make-up artist to Sarah Jessica Parker for various films including *The Family Stone* (2005) and *Did You Hear About the Morgans?* (2009)

2002 won an Oscar for her work on *Frida*, a film about the artist Frida Kahlo

2010–2011 leading make-up artist on *The Tempest* starring Helen Mirren

2011 nominated for a BAFTA for *Black Swan*

JET SET JOB

Being a celebrity make-up artist means working in an exciting and creative industry where no two days are the same. Here are just a few reasons why you might want to pick up your brushes and give it a try.

1 If you want a career full of variety with no two days the same, be a make-up artist! You'll be thrust into a world where there is little routine. Some jobs might take you on location to glamorous film sets, while others mean working in photographic studios. With such variety, you will be a world away from the daily grind of a 9–5 office job.

2 You'll get to work with the most creative people in the business. Three or four talented make-up artists work together backstage at fashion shows to follow the designer's brief. And if you're hired for a fantasy film, you could be one of ten artists! So, if you enjoy meeting new people and being a team player, this could be the ideal career for you.

3 Most make-up artists are 'freelance'. This means you work for yourself, rather than an organisation. As a result, you decide if the job, time and place interest you. You also get to choose your work and who you work with. As your own boss, you manage your own time and sieze the opportunities that come your way.

4 Top make-up artists are invited to film screenings and post-prémiere parties, so you could socialise with the stars whose make-up you have just created. Just like them, your name will be on the film's credits. If the make-up is central to the look of the film, you could even make a name for yourself as a star and then it could be *you* on stage accepting an award!

If you get to the top of your game, you could be invited to create a brand new image for stars such as Rihanna.

HANNAH MURRAY

THE STATS

Name: Hannah Murray
Born: 30 January 1979
Nationality: British
Based in: London

Early dreams

As a young girl, Hannah dreamed of being a ballerina. With years of training, she made her dream come true and became a professional dancer. Then, suddenly, she was forced to rethink her whole future when she injured her ankle. After three ankle operations, Hannah realised she would never dance again. Luckily, she had more than one talent – Hannah had always loved make-up and had made up the other dancers before shows. She decided that this could be her new career.

Make-up superstar

In 2010, Hannah was invited to become the make-up consultant for Topshop. She has helped to create new make-up ranges inspired by themes such as the Amazon, sandstorms and heavy metal. Today, Hannah travels the world, works with the best in the business, and has made her mark as a top make-up artist. In constant demand by fashion houses, magazines and superstars, and with her passport and kitbag ever ready, Hannah Murray is one of the hottest global artists.

Big break

In 1998, at just 19 years old, Hannah studied on an eight-week course at the famous Glauca Rossi School of Make-up in London, UK. Her big break was when she became first assistant to one of the world's leading make-up artists, Charlotte Tilbury. Hannah spent two years with Charlotte, working with her every day and travelling the world while she learnt about the business.

Cover girl

After her demanding schedule with Charlotte, Hannah had learnt enough to launch her own career. In 2006, she was the make-up artist for the Flash Louis cover for *i-D Magazine*. Two years later, she made up Victoria Beckham for the star's first cover shoot for British *Vogue*. Since 2008, Hannah has styled dozens of covers for magazines including British, Italian and French *Vogue*. She has worked with some of the world's top photographers including Patrick Demarchelier, Nick Knight and Mario Testino, and made up celebrities such as Alexa Chung and Lady Gaga.

MAKING A DIFFERENCE

Not content to stay behind the scenes in the dressing room, a few celebrity make-up artists are using cosmetics to make a difference.

Eco-aware

Getting a great look that is also environmentally friendly is fast becoming the style of many make-up artists. With increased awareness of natural products and organic ingredients, many artists are turning their backs on the chemical-filled creams and applications of the past.

Celebrity make-up artist Lina Hanson is one of a growing number of artists who use only eco-friendly products. Her eco-aware A-list clients include Naomi Watts, Mandy Moore and Zac Efron.

Made with minerals

One of the most recent trends in modern make-up is the use of minerals to create 'pure', chemical-free make-up that does not block skin pores. The company Bare Escentuals started the concept with their range of mineral-based powders, Bare Minerals. The brand describe the range as 'make-up so pure you can sleep in it' and have a celebrity fan base ranging from Jennifer Aniston to Natalie Portman. The brand proved so popular that other

Many celebrities, including Zac Efron (left), are fans of organic cosmetics and skin-friendly mineral make-up (above).

cosmetic giants, such as L'Oréal and MAC, have since launched their own mineral-based make-up ranges.

Life beyond lipstick

Bobbi Brown is a hugely successful American make-up consultant and author, who tries to make a difference with her charity work. Through 'Dress for Success', Bobbi provides underprivileged women with clothes and make-overs to help give them the confidence to attend job interviews.

Whether it's improving people's lives or protecting the planet, today the cosmetics industry is showing that make-up really can make a difference.

BEAUTY BANTER

Give your vocab a make-over with the ultimate Radar guide!

bronzer
a powder or cream applied to the skin to give it a sun-kissed glow

call time
the time you need to be on set or in the studio, ready to work

character sheet
used on film and TV sets, this has all the key information about a character's look and personality

concealer
a cream or powder that covers up spots, scars and eye bags

foundation
powder or liquid that is applied before any make-up to give skin an even colour and to cover any blemishes

kitbag
a bag make-up artists use to store make-up and brushes when working on set

kohl
a black powder used as eye make-up

liquorice
the blackest shade of black for mascara and eye pencils

matte
natural looking make-up that is not glossy

palette
a collection of matching shades of eyeshadow, lipstick or blusher

portfolio
a paper or digital folder with photos of a make-up artist's previous work

prosthetic
a plastic attachment used to change an actor's appearance

shadow stick
a smooth eyeshadow used to create smoky eyes

tear stick
a special wax that has tear-making chemicals

False eyelashes and rich colours are used to create dramatic eyes.

toner
a liquid that is applied to the skin to remove cleanser and tighten skin pores. It is also part of a cleansing routine before and after make-up

touch-ups
final adjustments to make-up before the cameras roll

tear sheet
articles, pictures and images from magazines that are torn out for inspiration and ideas

undertone
the natural colours that lie beneath your skin. Make-up artists base their colour choices on a client's undertones

GLOSSARY

A-list
the most famous people in the entertainment and film industry

arsenic
a deadly poison

BAFTA
the British Academy of Film and Television Arts

end roll credits/ film credits
the list of actors and other professionals in a film, shown at the end of the film

fine art
a college course that focuses on how to create art as well as the history of art

flawless
perfect and unmarked in any way

freelance
when someone is self-employed and works for different companies on short-term contracts

henna
a reddish dye made from the powdered leaves of a plant

iconic
instantly recognisable and influential

latex
a type of rubber

lead
a soft, poisonous metal that is blue-grey in colour

prémiere
the first viewing of a film

timeless
something that does not date

vulgar
rude

wrap
the end of filming

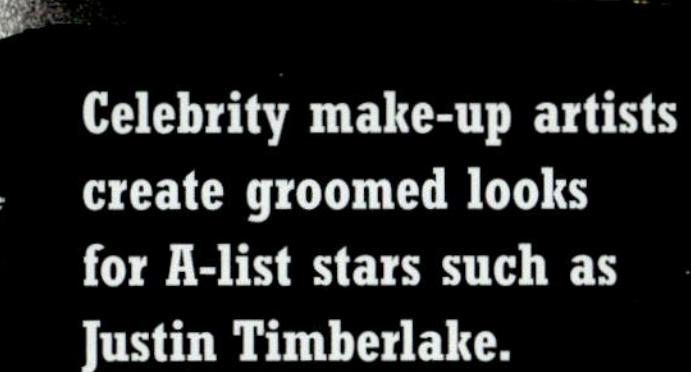

Celebrity make-up artists create groomed looks for A-list stars such as Justin Timberlake.

LOVELY LIPS!

Finish off the make-up look you began on pages 10–11 by making up your lips. Here's how to recreate Rihanna's perfect peachy pout!

You will need:

- peachy-coloured lip liner
- lipstick • lip gloss • lipstick brush

1 Begin by lining the lips with a peachy-coloured lip liner.

2 Use the lipstick brush to apply lipstick to the lips.

3 Apply lip gloss. This will add a sheer, shimmery finish to the lipstick.

Top tip

Using a brush to apply the lipstick will ensure that you get a perfectly smooth finish. Complete the look by applying a peachy-toned blusher to your cheekbones.

STAR MAKER

My story by Mimi D

Ever since I was a little girl, I have been fascinated by make-up. One day, my aunt gave me her favourite pink lipstick, and I decided there and then to turn my passion into a career and become a make-up artist.

I read everything I could about make-up, mostly by celebrity make-up artists such as Kevyn Aucoin and Laura Mercier. I tore out interesting articles on different types of make-up from magazines and kept them in a file. I still add tear sheets to my file even now.

I spent hours practising on friends and clients and kept a photographic record of the looks I created to build up my portfolio. I also worked for free to gain experience and contacts. I worked in make-up studios, fashion shops and on make-up counters, which was a great way to learn. I did a theatrical and media make-up course and then became the national trainer for a top French cosmetic company.

Now I work as a freelance make-up artist. One day I'll be doing a photo shoot for an advertising campaign, the next day, a private client's wedding. The following day, I might do a glamorous fashion show and then the next day, I might be making up a celebrity client. I can't leave the house without a suitcase and a travel bag – I take about 50 eyeshadows, and then about 20 of every other product!

The best thing about my job is that it never feels like a job. I'm my own boss, I have my own website, I work with artistic people and I get to be creative every day. One day, I'd love to do Madonna's make-up – so, if you see her, remember to give her my number!

REAL LIFE STORY

CENTURIES OF COSMETICS

For centuries, people have experimented with make-up and created dramatic looks using whatever ingredients they could find. Even poisonous ones…

All made up

The ancient Egyptians were all about 'Cleopatra eyes'! They used luminous green eyeshadow made from copper powder and heavy black lines made from a mixture of soot and kohl. Later, the Romans used chalk to whiten their faces and henna to colour their hair. They also used beetroot juice to create lipstick and blusher.

Strictly no tanning

In the Middle Ages, wealthy women covered their faces with lead paint or powder and wore pink lipstick, to show they could afford to buy cosmetics. Prostitutes, on the other hand, painted their faces pink to mark themselves out in a crowd and distinguish themselves from upper-class women.

Poisonous powder

In seventeenth century England, ladies painted their faces with white lead powder that contained arsenic. This caused their faces to pucker and scar so they put even more make-up on to cover it up.

Rude reds

In eighteenth century France, red lips were all the rage and represented health and fun. However, in nineteenth century England, Queen Victoria considered make-up 'vulgar' and suitable only for actresses and prostitutes!

Max Factor to wow-factor

The make-up created by Russian immigrant Max Factor was used in early Hollywood films to create a dramatic look for stars such as Rudolph Valentino. Today, the grandson of the make-up pioneer, Davis Factor, has invented his own brand, Smashbox, which creates cosmetics that aim to provide a flawless finish on-camera for the stars of today.

Today, make-up artists and the models they work with are credited with setting new trends for make-up looks that are followed by people around the world.

MITSUKI McCORMACK

Radar consultant Mitsuki McCormack has been a make-up artist to film stars and celebrities for ten years. We interviewed Mitsuki to find out all about her glamorous job.

What inspired you to become a make-up artist?

I was studying art and fashion but wasn't quite sure which career path was best for me. A friend introduced me to a make-up artist and I helped him at a fashion photo shoot. Straight away, I knew it was the job for me.

What's been your career highlight so far?

Working for celebrities is fun but being asked to create corpses for the film *Moon in Gemini* has taken my career into a great new area. Making people look hideous is just as much fun as making them look fabulous!

What is the best thing about your job?

I'm able to design new looks, work with artistic people, be as creative as I like – and I'm invited to film screenings. Seeing my name on the end roll credits really is the icing on the cake!

And the worst...?

I would say it's probably the long working hours. On average, I work ten-hour days, if not more (and often with no lunch break!), when I'm working on a film or TV set.

Which stars would you like to create a look for?

Top of the list are stars with expressive faces, such as Christina Ricci, who are both beautiful and open-minded about creating different looks.

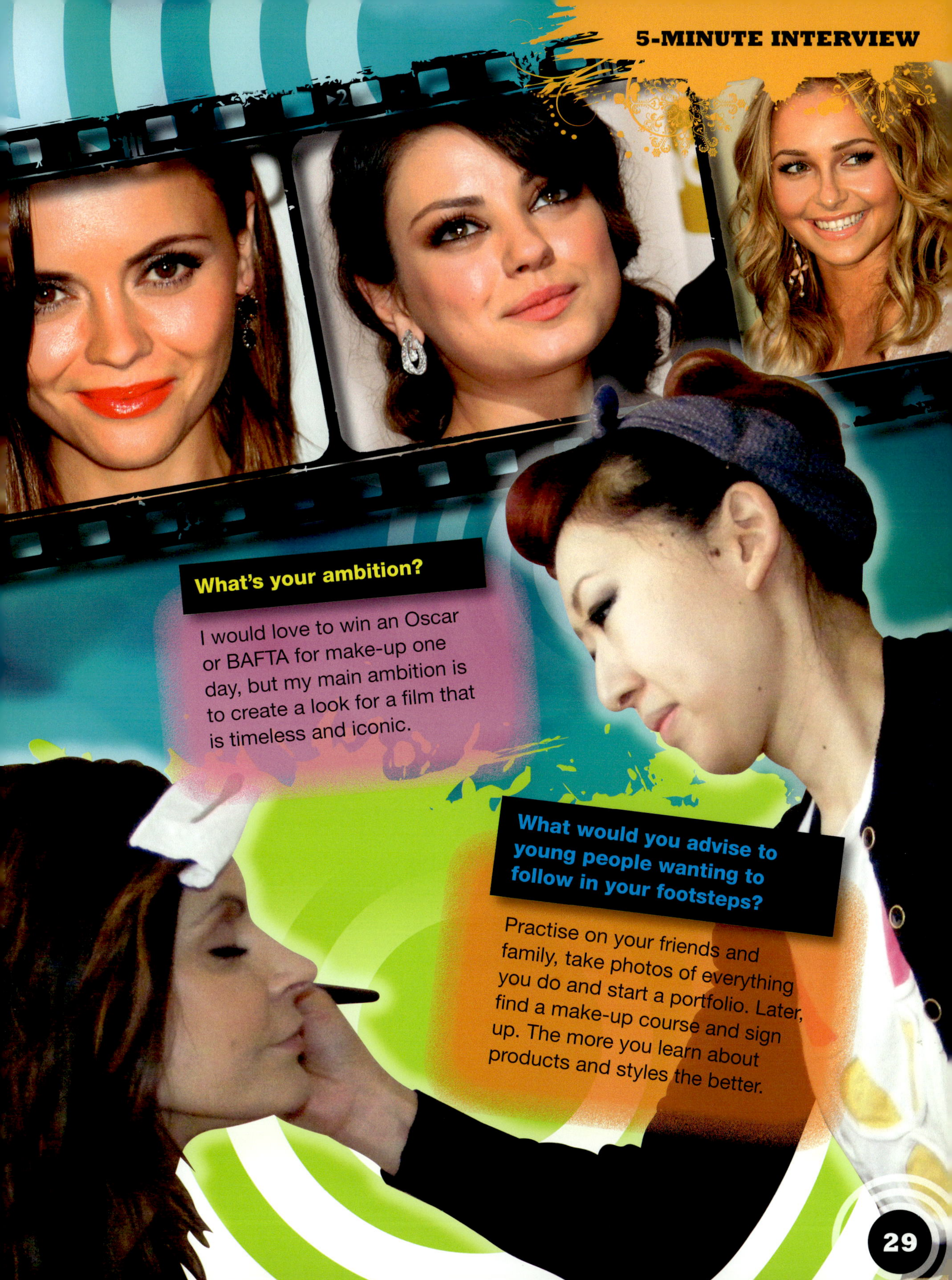

What's your ambition?

I would love to win an Oscar or BAFTA for make-up one day, but my main ambition is to create a look for a film that is timeless and iconic.

What would you advise to young people wanting to follow in your footsteps?

Practise on your friends and family, take photos of everything you do and start a portfolio. Later, find a make-up course and sign up. The more you learn about products and styles the better.

TOOLBAG TIPS

There are no lengths a true celebrity make-up artist will not go to in order to achieve the perfect look for their client. Here are the professional make-up artists' top ticks of the trade.

1. Sparkling eyes

Make-up artists never go anywhere without teabags! When wet, they make fantastic eyepads and help to restore A-list sparkle to tired eyes. If put in the fridge for five minutes before use, they also cool and freshen sore eyes.

2. Top brushes

A great make-up artist invests in top quality make-up brushes. Many make-up artists buy some of their brushes from art shops because of the superb quality of their brush fibres.

3. Gorgeous lips

Before applying lipstick or lipgloss, make-up artists prepare the lips by rubbing them with a toothbrush dipped in a little water and sugar. This removes any flaky skin and plumps up the lips so that any lipstick then applied does not crease or crack.

4. Perfect base

All make-up artists insist on working with perfectly cleansed and smooth skin. If an artist has no exfoliator to hand, sugar makes a fantastic dead skin remover. The make-up artist pours a little white sugar into the palm of the hand, mixes with a few drops of water, then rubs the homemade exfoliator onto the skin. Rough skin is removed and the complexion is given an instant pink glow.

5. Tub of magic

Many make-up artists swear by vaseline – it has a multitude of uses. It can be used to soothe dry and chapped skin and is ideal for holding groomed eyebrows in place. Last, but not least, it can be used as a slick of gloss over lipstick to create a luscious, perfect pout.

MAKE-UP MATTERS

Blusher, lipstick, brushes – check! Once you have the equipment, start practising on your family and friends and give them the red carpet treatment! Experiment, invent and create bold new looks and take photos for your portfolio. Radar also recommends:

People to talk to

Radar celebrity make-up consultant Mitsuki McCormack is on-hand to answer your questions if you want to be a make-up artist. Contact her at: **www.mitsukimccormack.webs.com**

Have a look at Mimi D's website to see the range and variety in the work of a freelance make-up artist: **www.mimidmakeup.com**

Check out Radar celebrity make-up artist Cassie Lomas' courses at: **www.cassielomasmakeupacademy.co.uk**

Find the very latest make-up tips at: **www.teenvogue.com**

Reads & Apps

About Face: Celebrity Makeup Techniques by Scott Barnes (Apple Press, 2010)

The Complete Make-up Artist: Working in Film, Fashion, Television and Theatre by Penny Delamar (WWTW, 2002)

Try out the *MakeUp* and *Celebrity Makeup Looks* apps, both are available at: **www.itunes.com** **https://market.android.com**

INDEX

Get more hot topic reads!

Celebrity Photographer

Celebrity Stylist

Being a Model

Street Dance

Bhangra & Bollywood

Capoeira

Ice Dancing

Latin Dance

The Armed Services

The Special Forces

Undercover Operations

Police Forensics